Back in Time

Living and Working in Ancient Rome

Edited by
Joanne Randolph

Enslow Publishing
101 W. 23rd Street
Suite 240
New York, NY 10011
USA
enslow.com

This edition published in 2018 by:
Enslow Publishing, LLC.
101 W. 23rd Street, Suite 240
New York, NY 10011

Library of Congress Cataloging-in-Publication Date

Names: Randolph, Joanne, editor.
Title: Living and working in ancient Rome / edited by Joanne Randolph.
Description: New York, NY : Enslow Publishing, [2018] | Series: Back in time | Includes bibliographical references and index. | Audience: Grades 3-6.
Identifiers: LCCN 2017001856| | ISBN 9780766089754 (library bound book) | ISBN 9780766089730 (pbk book) ISBN 9780766089747 (6 pack)
Subjects: LCSH: Rome—Civilization—Juvenile literature. |Rome—History—Juvenile literature.
Classification: LCC DG77 .L58 2016 | DDC 937—dc23
LC record available at https://lccn.loc.gov/2017001856

Printed in the United States of America

To Our Readers: We have done our best to make sure all website addresses in this book were active and appropriate when we went to press. However, the author and the publisher have no control over and assume no liability for the material available on those websites or on any websites they may link to. Any comments or suggestions can be sent by e-mail to customerservice@enslow.com.

Photos Credits: Cover, p. 1 Samot/Shutterstock.com; series logo, jeedlove/Shutterstock.com; back cover, Reinhold Leitner/Shutterstock.com; hourglass on spine, MilaLiu/Shutterstock.com; pp. 4, 12, 17, 22, 36 Andrey Yurlov/Shutterstock.com; p. 5 Peter Hermes Furian/Shutterstock.com; pp. 6, 7, 10-11 Culture Club/Hulton Archive/Getty Images; pp. 8-9 DEA/G. Nimatallah/De Agostini/Getty Images; pp. 13, 34 DEA Picture Library/De Agostini/Getty Images; pp. 14, 41 DEA/G. Dagli Orti/De Agostini/Getty Images; pp. 16, 42 Heritage Images/Hulton Archive/Getty Images; p. 18 Stock Montage/Archive Photos/Getty Images; p. 20 DEA/C. Sappa/De Agostini/Getty Images; p. 23 ullstein bild/Getty Images; p. 27 Rita K/Shutterstock.com; p. 30 Cultura RM Exclusive/Tim E White/Getty Images; p. 31 DEA/A. De Gregorio/De Agostini Picture Library; p. 35 Print Collector/Hulton Archive/Getty Images; p. 37 Chris Hill/Shutterstock.com; p. 38 Universal Images Group/Getty Images.

Article Credits: Cyndy Hall, "Take a Walk in Ancient Rome,"*AppleSeeds*; Anthony Hollingsworth, "Let's Meet," *Dig Into History*; Joann Burch, "Dormice for Dinner," *Dig Into History*; Mark Rose, "An Obelisk at the Hippodrome," *Dig Into History*; Elizabeth Fraccaro, "An Emperor's Prize," *Dig Into History*; Angela Murock Hussein, "A Riot," *Dig Into History*; Angela Murock Hussein, "A Royal City," *Dig Into History*; Anthony Hollingsworth, "Let's Visit El Djem," *Dig Into History*; Kenneth G. Holum, "An Archaeologist's Dream," *Dig Into History*.

CONTENTS

CHAPTER 1

WELCOME TO ANCIENT ROME

Rome, the City of Seven Hills, was a busy, crowded city two thousand years ago. It was the heart of the Roman Empire, lands controlled by Rome across Europe and into Asia and Africa.

In ancient times, most Romans began their day at sunrise. Slaves served heaping platters of wine-soaked bread, olives, cheese, and fruit to wealthy citizens reclining on cushions set out in the courtyards of their villas. On the streets, workmen and schoolboys bought rolled-up pancakes or thick slices of dark bread at bakeries. Poor and unemployed Romans lined up to receive the government's daily distribution of free bread on the street called Via Sacra.

This map shows how far the Roman Empire and its civilization spread at its height.

Streets were crowded with men. Most women stayed at home, taking care of their house and family. Most of the men walked everywhere, because the government banned wheeled vehicles from sunrise until late afternoon. Slaves carried wealthy citizens high above the crowds on covered litters.

A Busy Place

Noise was everywhere. Workers and shopkeepers cranked open the heavy shutters that protected their workshops and stores, then carried benches and tables loaded with goods to the open sidewalk. Soldiers wearing leather or chain-mail armor strode past workmen laying

The market was a busy place with lots of people coming to talk and buy goods in the shops.

water pipes or constructing a new apartment building. Teachers and students recited lessons behind curtained alcoves, shouting over the sounds of goldbeaters, carpenters, boilermakers, barbers, moneychangers, and furniture craftsmen. Street vendors carrying sausages and puddings on trays that were balanced on their heads yelled up to women leaning against the open windowsills of their apartments. The followers of Bellona, the goddess of war, chanted and sang as they made their way to the Forum. (Like the Greeks, Romans worshipped gods and goddesses.)

AT THE FORUM

The Roman Forum was the main business and political center of the city. Many Roman citizens spent their mornings at the Forum. Great speakers debated for hours at the Forum's comitium, an open space where people gathered. Citizens listened for a few minutes, then wandered across the open space to do their banking or trading. Businessmen made deals, financiers discussed loans, and moneychangers jingled coins in their hands to attract the attention of customers.

Others prayed and left offerings at temples dedicated to one of their many gods. In the nearby offices of the Roman Empire, senators and government officials argued over affairs of state. Through the open windows of the courts, the loud voices of lawyers arguing their clients' cases mixed with the shouts and laughter of spectators.

Outside, a heated argument sometimes became a noisy street fight. Priests and temple musicians led long funeral processions through the crowds. Thieves watched for opportunities from hidden spots in the shadows.

This overhead view of the Roman Forum shows the many temples and government buildings where officials made decisions about the government and court cases were heard.

AFTERNOON BREAK

In the afternoons, most Romans took time to rest and eat a cold midday meal at home. Shops closed, students walked home for a two- to three-hour break from school, and the streets were deserted. Only slaves and the poorest Romans worked through the midday break. The average family ate a simple dinner of vegetables and fruit at home. Sometimes wealthy merchants and nobles hosted large dinner parties—for men only.

Evening Entertainment

In the evening, the people of ancient Rome headed for large open-air theaters, the Colosseum, or the Circus Maximus. Because most performances were free, poor people enjoyed the same entertainment as did the wealthy.

If wealthy Romans stayed home, they lit oil lamps at sunset. If the poor stayed home, they went to bed at dark. Oil was expensive!

Visitors walking the streets of Rome for the first time found new adventures of sight, sound, and smell around every corner. Yes, it was loud, dirty, and sometimes dangerous—but no one cared. After all, Rome was the heart of the greatest empire in the world. How could anything be more exciting than that?

Dormice for Dinner

Have you ever wondered what children in ancient Rome ate? Pizza? Pasta? No. Those foods weren't invented two thousand years ago. How about vegetables? Yes. They ate celery and asparagus, turnips and carrots, beans and peas. But there were no potatoes, corn, or tomatoes. These vegetables came much later from America. And, instead of milk from cows, Roman children drank milk from sheep and goats.

A favorite Roman dish was dormice stuffed with pork and pine kernels, then cooked in honey and poppy seeds. Dormice were rodents about the size of a squirrel. They

The Colosseum is the largest amphitheater ever built, seating up to eighty thousand people. An amphitheater is an open-air place for entertainment, such as theater or sports.

were kept in cages and fattened before being ready to eat. Only rich people ate dormice, however. This was a special dish. Other special dishes were peacock brains, flamingo tongues, and milk-fed snails.

The people of ancient Rome ate very little during the day. Breakfast was often a piece of bread rubbed with garlic, and a glass of water.

Lunch for the poor was usually more bread. The rich didn't eat much for lunch either: cheese, fruit, and bread dipped in wine.

Dinner was the big meal of the day. Ordinary people ate bread and beans, cabbage, or vegetable soup. If they were lucky, they had a little meat.

Everything was cooked in one pot, and the whole family dug in with their fingers. Romans didn't eat with forks and spoons.

The rich ate with their fingers, too, but they used spoons to serve themselves and knives to cut their meat. Instead of forks, toothpicks were used to pick up food. Of course, eating this way made fingers very sticky. On the table were bowls of water for cleaning their hands. Dinner was served in three courses: First there were olives or anchovies, vegetables, and herbs. Next came a meat dish, such as roasted baby goat, ostrich, venison, or sometimes salted fish. Then it was time for dessert, which was usually fresh fruit—grapes, figs, plums, or apples.

This illustration shows Romans enjoying dinner in their garden. You can see that people often laid down to eat and there might be musicians playing music during the meal.

CHAPTER 2

THE ROMAN BATHS

Where do you and your family meet with friends? At the park? At the mall? At the baseball or soccer field? Well, two thousand years ago, the rich and the poor, as well as the young and the old, began their day with a visit to the baths. For all Romans, the public baths were the city's community center. They loved to gossip and discuss current events, and they did not bathe or shower in their houses, as very few houses had such facilities. Thus, the public baths became the perfect place to do both.

LET'S TAKE A LOOK

A visit to the baths would typically begin in a room called the tepidarium. Partially heated and often connected to a workout area, the tepidarium was a place to stretch and warm up. Visitors then entered the very hot room or caldarium. Here, they would sit on benches, naked, or swim in the hot pools. The Romans believed that sweating cleansed the body. The caldarium is one of those engineering marvels that we credit to Roman civilization. The floors in these rooms sat upon pillars several feet off of the ground. Hot air from the furnaces circulated between the floors, around the pillars, heating the room and pools. The floors were so hot, the Romans needed to wear wooden slippers to walk around. After scraping off the sweat with a tool called the strigilis, visitors entered the frigidarium, where they would cool down before leaving.

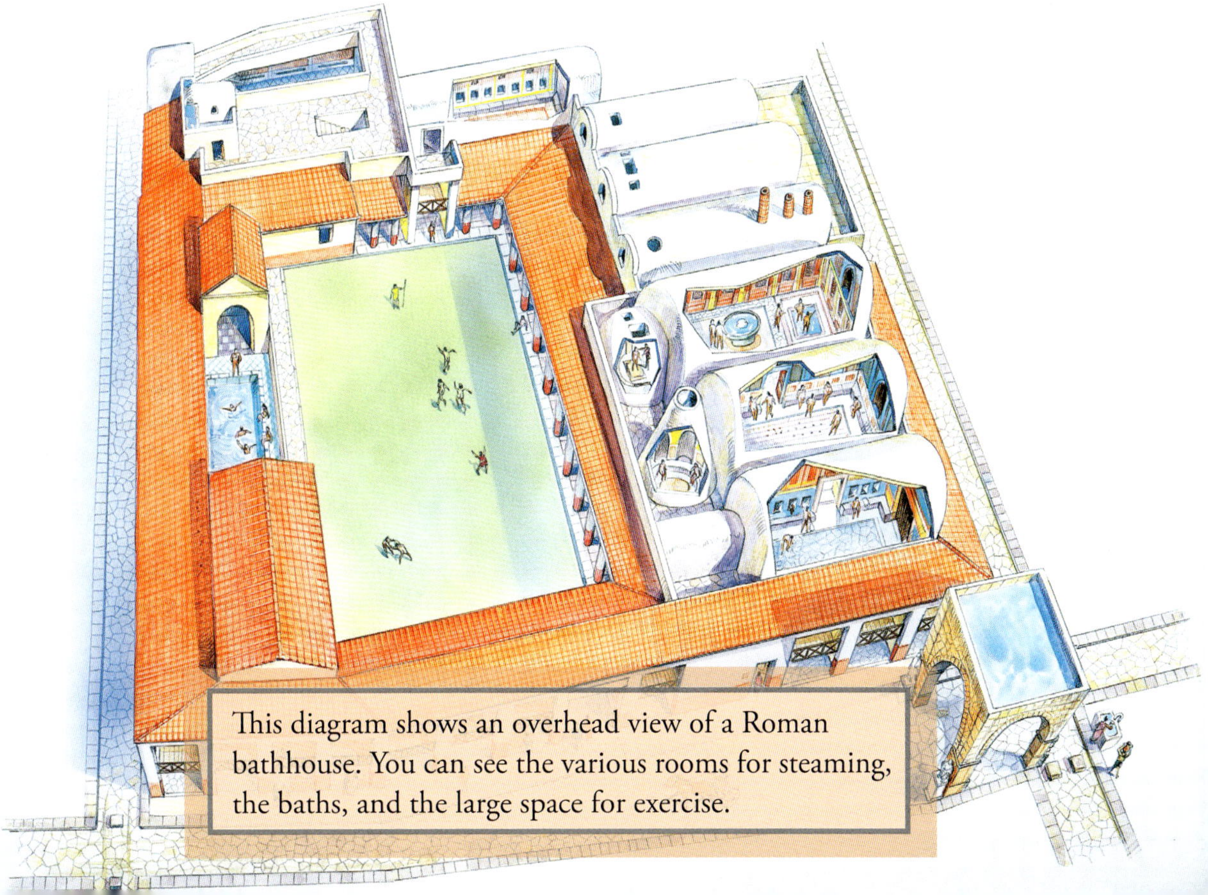

This diagram shows an overhead view of a Roman bathhouse. You can see the various rooms for steaming, the baths, and the large space for exercise.

In Byzantium (ancient Istanbul in Turkey), which was part of ancient Rome, archaeologists have discovered at least eight large public baths and at least 150 smaller ones, probably for private use. Some of them are no larger than a three-room building, while others are enormous. But the most important were the Baths of Zeuxippus, which means "the sacred area of Zeus." These were built at the end of the second century CE by the emperor Septimius Severus and stood where a temple to Zeus had once been.

BIGGER AND BETTER

For one hundred years, the Baths of Zeuxippus, like all Roman baths, stood out as an engineering wonder. But, in the third century, under Emperor Constantine, they became something more. They became the center of a vast complex of racetracks, forums, marketplaces, and palaces. Constantine had just taken control of the Roman Empire, the armies of the west had been defeated, and the city of Rome had lost much of its power. This new emperor wanted to make Byzantium the new center of the Roman Empire. He wanted it to be the new Rome.

This image shows the frigidarium, or the room where Romans would go to cool down before leaving the baths, at the baths near the Stabian Gate in Pompeii.

How do you make a city the most important city in an empire? Constantine started by renaming it Constantinople. After all, the most significant city is probably the one named after its most important citizen! Next, he built markets, palaces, and gaming areas for the people. He also enlarged the famed Hippodrome, so it seated one hundred thousand spectators. He rebuilt the Augustaion, a huge public square that served as the food market, and built a private residence for himself that came to be called the "Great Palace." At the center of all these massive structures and connected to all of them were the Baths of Zeuxippus.

A New Vision

Shopping, entertainment, athletics, and politics were not the only activities that took place around the vast complex of buildings. Constantine's vision of the new capital went much further. He also wanted his city center to be inspirational, and the Baths of Zeuxippus again played a major role in his plans. Ever since the first-century BCE, when the Roman poet Vergil wrote about the Trojan War, Romans had considered their city the second Troy. Constantine knew these legends and saw his city as the third Troy. Constantine also wanted the people to recognize Rome's heroes as their own ancestors. He achieved these goals by erecting statues of Trojan heroes, Greek poets, and Roman rulers throughout the baths. If you want people to achieve greatness, Constantine thought, you need to expose them to great models. Since everyone went to the baths daily, they offered the perfect place to display these statues. Every day, Romans entering the baths were greeted by the likes of the poet Homer, the Trojan hero Hector, the philosopher Aristotle, and, of course, the Roman general and statesman Julius Caesar.

This statue of Constantine stands outside a church in North Yorkshire, England. The town was an important military base for the Roman empire.

Unfortunately, very little of these baths or the statues that once stood there remain. Archaeologists have unearthed the bases of several statues, and some of the excavated areas indicate a space for groups of statues. But our only detailed source on these sculptures comes from an Egyptian poet named Christodorus of Coptos. Living nearly two centuries after Constantine transformed the city, Christodorus wrote poems about eighty of the statues. "And, next to the others," Christodorus wrote of Julius Caesar, "I saw the man who long ago decorated Rome with the shields of her enemy and held the title of the second Zeus."

The Roman baths are testimony to Roman engineering genius and love of functional architecture. The Baths of Zeuxippus took Roman ingenuity to the next level. Not only were these baths practical, they were also educational and served as the focal point of Constantinople. They definitely were the hub of Constantine's perfect city.

CHAPTER 3

REMINDERS OF CONQUESTS

What's an Egyptian obelisk doing in the middle of Istanbul? For the answer, we must look to Augustus, a Roman emperor who ruled about three hundred years before Constantine. In 10 BCE, the trend-setting Augustus ordered that an obelisk be placed in the Circus Maximus, the stadium where chariot races were held in Rome. The tall stone pillar he had brought from Heliopolis in Egypt would constantly remind the 150,000 spectators who crowded in to watch the races of how Augustus had conquered Egypt. It was a classic example of appropriation. The Romans were good at this, as they often took a monument from a conquered city or culture as a trophy.

THE SPINA ON PARADE

In ancient Constantinople, chariot races were the most popular pastime. They took place in the Hippodrome, which actually was much more than a racetrack. It was also a vast stage for political spectacle and national mythology. During a race, chariots circled a narrow barrier, known as the *spina*, which ran down the center of the course. As in the Circus Maximus, the spina in the Hippodrome was decorated with monuments honoring historical triumphs. On display as well, in a special box-seat area, known as the *kathisma*, were members of the imperial family, who wanted crowds to see

This engraving shows the Hippodrome in Constantinople. In the center of the picture are the many obelisks and trophies that celebrated the Romans' victories over others.

them as representing the state's present and future greatness. To this day, the center of the Hippodrome is marked by an obelisk.

Originally, the Hippodrome's obelisk stood in the temple of Amun-Re at Karnak in Egypt. It had been commissioned by Thutmose III, who ruled from 1472 to 1457 BCE, to commemorate his crossing the Euphrates River "with valor and victory at the head of his army." The Roman emperor Theodosius I, who ruled from 378 to 392 CE, had it brought to the Hippodrome and positioned it on a marble pedestal. The reliefs carved into the pedestal show Theodosius overseeing the raising of the obelisk and looking down at captives who kneel before him. One relief shows him with his family, watching a race. In another, he is between his sons Honorius and Arcadius and crowning a victorious charioteer. An inscription proudly proclaims that "all things yield to Theodosius and to his everlasting descendants."

A "Stage" for Monuments

The obelisk was not the first impressive monument set in the Hippodrome. Another was a serpent column Constantine had brought from Delphi in Greece. After the Greeks defeated the Persians in 479 BCE, they dedicated to the god Apollo a gold tripod. Beneath it, as a support, was a bronze column made in the form of three intertwined snakes. This column was cast from the weapons the Greeks took from the defeated Persians. Inscribed on the column was the phrase, in Greek, "Those who fought the war." Listed below were the names of the thirty-one city-states whose heroic troops saved Greece from Persian conquest.

The base of the serpent column at the Hippodrome still stands there today.

For Constantine, the column in the Hippodrome told all who saw it that Constantinople was the new Rome and that it now was responsible for protecting civilization from barbarian peoples. The serpent column remained intact until 1700, when the three snakeheads came crashing down. Today, one is preserved in Istanbul's Archaeology Museum.

THE TALE OF A DONKEY

One of the oddest monuments ever to be displayed in the Hippodrome was put there by Constantine. It came from Nikopolis in northwestern Greece. Augustus had founded this town to commemorate his 31 BCE victory over Mark Antony and Cleopatra. To further honor the event, especially the fact that Egypt was now part of the Roman World, Augustus commissioned a huge memorial that would incorporate into its design the bronze battering rams that had been cut from his enemy's ships. The memorial was to include a donkey, carrying a heavy load and braying, and his master. Why?

On the eve of the battle against Antony and Cleopatra, Octavius, as Augustus was known then, was gazing at the enemy's troops when a man and donkey came toward him. The man introduced himself as Eutyches, which translates to "Prosper," and his donkey as Nikon, which translates "Victory." He then told Octavius that he and his donkey were going to the victor's camp. Octavius saw this as a good omen and immortalized the pair in bronze. Well, almost immortalized them! The crusaders, who sacked Constantinople in 1204, destroyed the donkey.

CHAPTER 4

SOME ANCIENT ROMAN CITIES

About two thousand years ago, the city of Rome was the center of the Roman Empire, controlling land and people from Britain to Egypt. There was a distance of about 3,000 miles (4,828 kilometers) between the empire's farthest points. To travel across the empire on horseback would have taken almost one hundred days. Paved roads linked the whole empire together. The Roman roads were built so well that you can still travel many of them today. Let's take a look at some of the cities that were once part of the vast Roman Empire.

Caesarea Maritima

Caesarea Maritima—Caesar's City by the Sea—is a beautiful city and harbor that prospered for more than one thousand years, through invasions and wars, sweeping religious changes, economic crises, and the rule of cruel monarchs. It is a dream spot for ancient discoveries.

Archaeologists have spent lots of time excavating at Caesarea to gain insight into what life was like in ancient times.

The ruins of Caesarea Maritima can be seen in the foreground of this picture. Today, this city is part of Israel.

In the Beginning

Archaeologists discovered only a little about the first settlement on the site. A small town named Straton's Tower, it was founded in the third century BCE, perhaps as a seaport. Within two hundred years, it had fallen into decay and was abandoned. The inhabitants, who probably spoke Greek, worshiped Aphrodite, the Greek goddess of love, who was also known as Isis, an Egyptian goddess of sailors. They think the temple of Aphrodite–Isis stood on a rocky outcrop above the harbor, but have found little trace of it. The real builder of Caesarea was Herod the Great, who ruled from 37 BCE to 4 BCE.

A proud and cruel monarch and a friend of the Roman emperor Caesar Augustus, Herod also sought fame as a builder. Among his most impressive achievements was the city of Caesarea, which he founded above the ruins of Straton's Tower and named for Caesar Augustus. Next to the city, Herod built a huge harbor and named it Sebastos, Greek for "Augustus." Divers have explored the harbor over many years, studying the huge north and south breakwaters now sunk beneath the sea. In Herod's time, they enclosed a spacious harbor basin, and, on either side of the harbor entrance, stone towers supported colossal statues of imperial family members. What came as a surprise was the discovery that Herod's engineers and builders had constructed the break-waters mostly of hydraulic concrete that hardened underwater.

A Temple to the Gods

Rising above the harbor to the east was the stony ridge on which the temple of Aphrodite had once stood. Herod ordered the expansion of this ridge and had it surrounded with earth contained in massive retaining walls. On top he built a temple dedicated to Roma, the goddess of Rome, and Augustus, her temple-mate. The Romans honored the emperor Augustus as a god. While the divers excavated the harbor, the land archaeologists uncovered the foundations of Herod's temple, along with enough bits and pieces to put together the building itself with the help of a computer. It was a huge building, reaching more than 100 feet (30.5 meters) above the stony ridge. Within were two colossal statues, representing Roma and Augustus.

The streets in Herod's city were laid out in the Greek fashion, on a grid plan at right angles to one another. Houses and markets were all enclosed within fortification walls. As with other cities of the period, Caesarea had a generous supply of fresh water, probably from wells dug into the sandy soil. Beneath the streets was an elaborate stone sewer system that carried away rainwater and refuse. Herod also built a palace jutting into the sea, the so-called Promontory Palace, and nearby, a theater and amphitheater or hippodrome for the spectacles that would help him maintain his popularity with the citizens. Today, the theater often serves as the setting for rock concerts and operas—another reason for Caesarea's popularity with twenty-first-century visitors!

The City Goes Roman

Within years after Herod's death in 4 BCE, Roman governors ruled the area and named Caesarea the provincial capital. Soon, Latin became the official language. In 66 CE, the Jews of the province rebelled and a bloody war followed, one that ended with the destruction of Jerusalem in 70 CE. Early in this war, the commanding Roman general, Vespasian, stationed his legions in Caesarea. It was there that his legions proclaimed him the new Roman emperor. In gratitude, Vespasian re-founded Caesarea as a Roman colony, thereby granting the citizens of the city Roman citizenship.

The Romans did commission building projects, including a great aqueduct, but they neglected the harbor. Prosperity now depended more on the farms and ranches in the countryside that supplied the city with food. Fish remained a part of the diet, but it came from fish-farms, similar to modern ones. Ships still called at Caesarea, delivering goods from abroad and loading cargoes of wine, olive oil, and grain for export. But they used smaller anchorages at Caesarea or along the coast, or they anchored offshore and unloaded their cargoes into small boats that could land on the beaches. We know about this lively trade from finds of broken pottery, literally mountains of jars that once contained oil, wine, and other products.

The City Goes Christian

Change came in the 330s CE, when the Romans began to abandon their old gods to become Christians—all inspired by Constantine, the first Christian Roman emperor. Excavated finds have revealed, however, that Caesarea did not adopt Christianity until around 400, when Christians pulled down the temple to Roma and Augustus and the columns that surrounded it. They even dug out most of the foundations. Around 490, the Christian majority built a beautiful church on the same spot, octagonal in design, clothed in slabs of multicolored marble, and probably topped with a magnificent dome.

Caesarea did not reach the heights of prosperity until the sixth century. By this time, Greek had again become the main language. New structures included a fortification wall to enclose the growing city and three new aqueducts to meet the increasing demand for water. Although exact numbers are unavailable, we estimate a population inside the walls of thirty thousand or so, plus three times that in the villages and farms of the countryside. At the height of the

Many statues and artifacts were uncovered by archaeologists at Caesarea Maritima. They are now on display in the Caesarea Maritima National Park in Israel.

city's prosperity, the wealthiest citizens owned farms and ranches outside the city. They lived in sumptuous mansions within the city or in nearby villas, all decorated with mosaic pavements, marble columns and wall panels, and beautiful furniture. An example of this furniture is a recently discovered dining table decorated with gold-glass. The wealthy also wore robes of silk in many colors, and often personal jewelry such as the belt ornaments of gold that excavators discovered in a trench, mixed in with the dirt.

LET'S VISIT EL DJEM

Two thousand years ago, millions of olive trees, not desert sand, filled the landscape of North Africa. The temperature was a little cooler, the soil was fertile and the climate was perfect for olive trees. From the farthest western province of Mauretania—modern-day Morocco—all the way to the eastern province of Africa Proconsularis—modern-day Tunisia—farmers grew olive trees to harvest the oil from the olives. Used in the kitchen for cooking and at the gym for aching muscles, in oil lamps for light and even for medicine, African olive oil supplied the Roman markets and fed a hungry empire.

A GREAT TRADING CENTER

Today, when we think about computer companies, we think of Silicon Valley in California. When we think of the latest clothes fashions, Paris, France, comes to mind. From 100 CE until about 300 CE, when a Roman thought about olive oil, the town of Thysdrus in North Africa would have entered his thoughts. It was there that all the farmers sent their oil for sale and shipment. And, it is there that the wealth of ancient North Africa can still be seen. But do not try to find the city on a map, for it no longer goes by its ancient name. Today, it is known by its Arabic name, El Djem. Also, North Africa is not a present-day country. If you want to visit the archaeological site at Thysdrus, you must buy a ticket for Tunisia.

In the Roman Empire, as in all civilizations, some people were rich, some people were poor, and many were somewhere in the middle. The people in North Africa were no different, at least, not at first. When they started growing olive trees, everything changed. Farmers grew their olives, the presses turned them into oil, and the oil was sent to Rome. The wealth that flowed into these provinces pushed many farmers—even the poor ones—into the wealthiest class of Romans, and El Djem became the center of that wealth.

Rivaling Rome!

Much of the money that Thysdrus collected went to construct baths and houses for the city's residents and visitors. These structures gleamed white and housed some of the best ancient art that survives from Africa. But the jewel of the city was its amphitheater. It was 480 feet (146 m) long and 400 feet (123 m) wide, the largest structure the Romans ever built outside of Italy. Only the massive Colosseum in Rome, believed to have accommodated as many as forty thousand people, and the amphitheater in Capua, a city to the south of Rome, were larger.

The amphitheater at Thysdrus was built in 230 CE by the Roman governor Gordianus. Its size was no accident. Gordianus was sending the Roman emperor a message. Rome was growing weak, and the provinces were getting stronger. Even North Africa could have monuments rivaling those of Rome. In North Africa, ambition meant everything, and even the poorest farmer could become wealthy, with just hard work and an olive field.

The amphitheater at El Djem could seat around thirty-five thousand people. Many of its stones were taken to be used in buildings in El Djem and also the Great Mosque, but there are enough left to be able to imagine the amphitheater in the time of ancient Rome.

CONSTANTINOPLE AND A RIOT

During the reign of Justinian (527–565 CE), the city of Constantinople (modern-day Istanbul) reached, according to many, its peak. Yet, these years were not without losses. A plague swept through Constantinople during his reign, killing thousands of people. Wars and religious conflicts also took their toll. One of the greatest disasters to befall the city, however, was the result of a sporting event.

COME ONE, COME ALL!

In January of 532, Justinian arranged for a chariot race, an event that was intended to bring Constantinople's population together.

This mosaic showing Emperor Justinian is found in the Basilica of San Vitale in Ravenna, Italy.

Such competitions in the Byzantine Empire would be comparable to NASCAR and other major sporting events today. As with present-day halftime presentations, so these ancient events had circus acts between races. Since early Roman times, spectacles had been held on a grand scale to make rulers more popular with the people. And they did, especially since there was no admission fee. For Justinian, keeping his subjects in Constantinople happy was particularly important, since the taxes there were especially high.

Racing fans were divided into factions, with each group named after the color worn by its favorite chariot team. Their organization was similar to present-day soccer associations, social clubs, street gangs, and political parties—all rolled into one. People throughout the empire were particularly loyal to their teams, and competition between the factions was fierce. Sports riots were not uncommon occurrences in both Roman and Byzantine times.

Countering Unrest

In late 531, individuals from the Blues and the Greens were arrested for causing deaths in a riot in the city's Hippodrome after a race. A number of the hooligans were hanged. Two of them, however, one Blue and one Green, escaped death when the gallows broke just before it was their turn to be executed.

All the factions now united behind a common cause—protection of the convicted. They brought the two men to a church. According to custom—both at that time and, in many places, still today—sacred places offered protection to anyone, including fugitives. The people, no doubt stirred up by supporters of the different factions, demanded that the offenders be pardoned. Aware of the potential for civil unrest, the city's officials changed their sentences from death to imprisonment. This announcement was followed by another—there would be another chariot race.

The new race was meant to distract the city's populace from the fate of the two who had just escaped death, but events soon spun out of control. As the crowd arriving for the race streamed in, they became increasingly agitated, shouting insults at the palace and chanting Nika, which means "victory." Soon after, a frenzied riot broke out that lasted for five days. Eventually, the rioters were killed by troops loyal to the emperor. But the casualty count was horrific. The violence had caused an estimated thirty thousand deaths. The Nika riots had also led to more than half of Constantinople being destroyed by fire.

Architects at Work

Justinian was determined to rebuild the city on a grander scale. He wanted Constantinople to compare, even surpass, legendary cities of the past, places that were wonders to behold because of their efficient organization and their architectural beauty. He had the dwellings reconstructed with safer, more fire-resistant materials. He then had engineers design a system of roads and bridges to reduce traffic congestion.

Aware that fresh water is vital to keeping people healthy and clean, Justinian updated the aqueduct system, incorporating into its design an underground cistern. This reservoir was large enough to provide an uninterrupted supply of water to the city's inhabitants should they be attacked or experience a disaster. Its forest of columns and decorated ceiling arches and vaults was so vast that the structure's remains are known today as the "Sunken Palace."

Colonnades along the streets and public baths were rebuilt. The royal palace was beautified with several mosaics and a monumental gateway that boasted a shining bronze tile roof. There were also a new senate building, law school, orphanages, and hostels for

These columns are inside the Basilica Cistern, which was built to provide water to the palace and other buildings in Constantinople. It is the size of a cathedral.

The Hagia Sophia, or the Church of Santa Sophia, was built in Constantinople at the order of Justinian. Today it is a museum in modern-day Istanbul, Turkey.

travelers. During Justinian's reign, silkworms were smuggled out of China to Constantinople. Byzantine craftsmen then built facilities for the manufacture of silk cloth.

Even Today

Zoning laws were passed to make sure that construction did not take place within 100 feet (30.5 m) of the coastline, so as to ensure for all a magnificent view. Justinian also constructed or rebuilt more than thirty churches. The Church of the Holy Apostles, which had been dedicated by Constantine when he founded the city and was the burial place of the Byzantine emperors, was rebuilt on a grander scale. It housed a monumental burial place for Justinian and his family. The best-known reconstruction was the Church of Santa Sophia, an unrivaled architectural masterpiece even today.

SOME FAMOUS ROMANS

Lasting for around twelve centuries, ancient Rome was one of the largest ancient empires in the world. It is guessed that at points it had as many as ninety million subjects. A civilization that survived for that long had to have a number of famous historic figures, including thinkers, artists, and leaders. We will take a look at a few of the Romans who had a lasting impact on the civilization.

AUGUSTUS

Under Augustus' rule, the Pax Romana ("Roman Peace") prevailed. Trade and goodwill spread throughout the Roman Empire, whose boundaries now extended into modern-day Germany, Spain, France, and much of northern Africa. While a relatively peaceful time, these years had been ushered in by dramatic and often violent actions.

The Groundwork Set

This bust of Emperor Augustus was made during his lifetime. He did a great deal to improve the Roman Empire for his people, through changes in government, new building projects, and more.

Octavius was quite young—nineteen years old, to be exact—when he entered the deceitful world of Roman politics. Wanting to avenge the assassination of Julius Caesar, who had named him his heir, Octavius formed an alliance with two powerful Romans—Marc Antony and Lepidus. Together they suppressed the power of the Senate and defeated their enemies. Unfortunately, each of the three men sought to rule Rome. Lepidus was the first to be ousted from the alliance. After forcing him into exile, Antony and Octavius quickly divided the empire between them. Octavius took Rome, and Marc Antony took Egypt.

Upon learning that Marc Antony was in love with Egypt's queen, Cleopatra, many Romans feared that she would claim control of the Roman Empire for herself. They reasoned that she would do that with the help of Marc Antony. As for Octavius, he did not trust Marc Antony and so decided to attack Egypt before Antony and Cleopatra could strike at Rome. In 31 BCE, at the Battle of Actium, Octavius destroyed the Egyptian fleet and soon after captured Alexandria. Defeated, Antony and Cleopatra both committed suicide the following year. Octavius then annexed Egypt, and the Senate proposed that he assume a ten-year command of the Roman provinces that might be troublesome. One of these provinces was Egypt.

This engraving shows the sea battle at Actium, where Marc Antony and Cleopatra's combined forces were defeated by Octavius.

A Title with Power

Octavius' successful governance of the provinces prompted the Senate to give Octavius the title of Augustus (Latin for "illustrious one") in 27 BCE. This was not just a name; rather, it granted Octavius religious as well as political authority. Further, in giving Octavius this title, the Senate maintained an illusion of a free Republic whose political power continued to be in the hands of the Senate. But, in reality, the Senate was giving Octavius autocratic power, and the term was for life.

The province of Egypt, however, was not absorbed into the Roman Empire. Instead, it became part of Octavius' patrimonium—that is, his private property. The same policy was followed for every emperor who succeeded him. Octavius, in turn, rented land to the Egyptians, generating a huge sum of revenue. He used this money to finance his empire, including military expeditions and public works such as temples, theaters, roads, and aqueducts. He also used the funds to provide panem et circenses ("bread and games") that included extravagant entertainments such as gladiator fights. Another use for these funds was the distribution of free food, which pleased the Roman people and served to keep their loyalty. Such policies made Octavius genuinely popular with the Roman people, including the Roman citizens of Egypt.

Septimius Severus

It was the year 193 CE, and Rome had a new emperor. There had been many before him, but he was the first North African. Other emperors had been born beyond the boundaries of Rome, but not one had ever been African. The new emperor's name was Lucius Septimius Severus, and he was a general from the city of Leptis Magna.

Meet Severus

Severus had been born on April 11, 146, to a middle class family. In the late 160s, when he was in his early twenties, he immigrated to Rome, where he planned to pursue a career in public service. Under the emperor Marcus Aurelius, he held several of the traditional state offices, serving in such fields as law, administration, and finance. He also served as a public official in such diverse places as southern Spain, Sardinia, and Syria—all in addition to posts in his home province of Africa. When Marcus Aurelius died in 180, Severus went to Athens to study. Such travel was a common practice among wealthy Roman citizens at the time. Soon after, he was named governor of a region in Gaul (present-day France) and then Sicily.

Severus' next post was the governorship of Pannonia in Eastern Europe. While there, the Emperor Commodus was murdered. The year was 192, and the Roman Senate quickly chose Pertinax as the new emperor. Not everyone approved the choice, and just three months into his reign, he was assassinated by disgruntled Praetorians. At the time, Severus had control of the three legions stationed in the province where he was serving as governor. After hearing the news from Rome, he convinced his troops to support him in a bid for the imperial office. Two other governors did the same with their troops. But it was Severus who arrived in Rome first. The year was 193.

Septimius Severus did much to expand the Roman Empire through conquest. After he died due to an illness, he was succeeded by his sons as part of the Severan dynasty.

IN COMMAND

Severus was proclaimed emperor, and he acted quickly to consolidate support among the Praetorians and the Senate. He then left Rome to defeat rivals elsewhere. It would be four years before he returned. When he did, he turned his attention to making sure that he would have a lasting legacy. To honor the city of his birth, he ordered civic improvements that would make it one of the most spectacular cities of the empire.

The theater at Leptis Magna was first built in the first century CE, but Septimius Severus added to it during his reign.

But Severus was not the first emperor to beautify Leptis Magna. His predecessors had commissioned public buildings as well. They, too, recognized the importance of the area's many resources to the empire. They also believed that introducing every province to Roman culture would help to unify the vast empire with its many diverse peoples and languages. About eighty years earlier, the emperor Trajan had built a circus or chariot-racing course so that the citizens of Leptis Magna could enjoy traditional, Roman-style entertainment. Trajan's successor, Hadrian, had done much the same. Since bathing and athletics played a major role in Roman daily life, Hadrian had a large bath complex and gymnasium (part school, part gym) constructed.

A Grand Place

The people of Leptis Magna honored their rulers, as well as the imperial families, in the Temple of Rome and Augustus. Local officials and governors built arches to honor emperors such as Trajan.

Soon after Septimius Severus became emperor, Leptis Magna became the third most-important city in Africa, rivaling Carthage and Alexandria in its wealth. In 205, the imperial family visited the city, and a unique arch was erected to honor the visit.

A Vast Empire

As you can see, the Roman civilization was a vast one. Known for its beautiful cities, advanced technology, and culture, it is no wonder Ancient Roman civilization had a lasting impact on western civilization.

CHRONOLOGY

753 BCE The city of Rome is founded. Rome was ruled by kings for the next 240 years.

509 BCE Rome becomes a republic. Rome is now ruled by elected officials called senators.

45 BCE Julius Caesar becomes the first dictator of Rome.

44 BCE Julius Caesar is assassinated on the Ides of March by Marcus Brutus. They hope to bring back the republic, but civil war breaks out.

27 BCE The Roman Empire begins as Caesar Augustus becomes the first Roman emperor.

64 CE Much of Rome burns. Legend has it that Emperor Nero watched the city burn while playing a lyre.

80 CE The Colosseum is built.

306 CE Constantine becomes emperor. Constantine would convert to Christianity, and Rome would become a Christian empire.

380 CE Theodosius I declares Christianity to be the sole religion of the Roman Empire.

395 CE Rome splits into two empires, the Western Roman Empire and the Byzantine (Eastern Roman) Empire.

410 CE The Visigoths sack Rome.

476 CE The end of the Western Roman Empire and the fall of ancient Rome. The last Roman emperor, Romulus Augustus, is defeated by the German Goth Odoacer. This signals the start of the Dark Ages in Europe.

1453 CE The Byzantine Empire comes to an end as it falls to the Ottoman Empire.

GLOSSARY

amphitheater A round, roofless building with tiered seating for spectators to watch sports or other entertainment.

aqueduct A bridge created to carry water.

chariot A two-wheeled horse-drawn vehicle used in ancient warfare and racing.

citizen A legally recognized subject of a nation or commonwealth, especially one entitled to its privileges, such as the right to vote.

civilization The society, culture, and way of life of a particular area.

colonnades A row of columns often supporting a roof.

empire A collection of states or countries under the control of a single authority, such as an emperor or empress.

fortification A defensive wall or other structure built to defend a place against attack.

mosaic A picture or pattern created using small, colored bits of stone, tile, or glass.

obelisk A stone pillar that has a square or rectangular base and a pyramid-shaped top.

plague A contagious disease that causes fever, confusion, and sometimes other symptoms and spreads quickly through a population.

temple A structure used for worship or believed to be the home of a god or gods or their relics.

FURTHER READING

BOOKS

Baum, Margaux, and Julian Morgan. *Constantine.* New York, NY: Rosen Publishing, 2017.

Hamen, Susan E. *Ancient Rome.* Minneapolis, MN: Essential Library, 2015.

James, Simon. *DK Eyewitness Books: Ancient Rome.* London, UK: DK Children, 2015.

Kallen, Stuart A. *Life During the Roman Empire.* San Diego, CA: ReferencePoint Press, 2013.

Ridley, Sarah. *Life in Roman Times.* Mankato, MN: Smart Apple Media, 2016.

WEBSITES

History for Kids

www.historyforkids.net/ancient-rome.html

Dive deeper into the culture and history of ancient Rome.

Rome.info

www.rome.info/ancient/

Read a brief history of ancient Rome and view images and a map.

UShistory.org, Ancient Civilzations

www.ushistory.org/civ/6.asp

Discover more secrets of ancient Rome.

INDEX